Planner Belongs To:

_____

Thanksgiving Day Planner

Dedication

This Thanksgiving Planner book is dedicated to all the busy people who want to organize and prepare in the months leading up to the holiday.

You are my inspiration for producing this book and I'm honored to be a part of your Thanksgiving Day planning.

How to Use this Book

This Thanksgiving Journal will help guide you through every detail of planning your Thanksgiving festivities. It's a great way to plan and prepare in the months leading up to the Big Thanksgiving Feast.

Here are samples of daily and weekly calendars, checklists and more. Fill in and keep track of all the details:

1. Fill in calendar
2. Review checklist, mark when finished
3. Keep track of the budget
4. Fill in the cooking plan
5. Fill out the menu pages
6. Fill in your Master Ingredient list
7. Create your cooking schedule
8. Plan the table settings
9. Create the guest list
10. Jot down your favorite memories and save photos

Thanksgiving checklist

3 Weeks Before

Getting Organized

- ◯ Put all activities and appointments on the calendar.
- ◯ Set a budget for hosting Thanksgiving dinner.
- ◯ Create your guest list and invite your guests.
- ◯ Set RSVP date at least 10 days before Thanksgiving.

Plan The Menu

- ◯ Gather favorite Thanksgiving recipes and new recipes to try.
- ◯ Decide if you will make the entire meal yourself or ask guests to bring a dish.
- ◯ Plan your menu and create a comprehensive list of ingredients you'll need.

Preparing Your Kitchen

- ◯ Start a shopping list for all the food and supplies you'll need.
- ◯ Declutter countertops to make room for food preparations.
- ◯ Organize and inventory your pantry and freezer.
- ◯ Stock up on seasonal baking and cooking ingredients.

Preparing Your Home

- ◯ Plan your table décor and centerpiece. Take inventory of linens and accessories.
- ◯ Declutter and deep clean your dining room.
- ◯ Take stock of table and bar items using the checklist.
- ◯ Plan your Thanksgiving decor. Inspect candles and other decorations.
- ◯ Make a list of worn-out decorations or new décor to purchase.
- ◯ Take care of any home maintenance issues or "spruce up" areas in need.

Notes

Notes

Thanksgiving *checklist*

Sunday/Monday

- ◯ Confirm guest attendance and food contributions.
- ◯ Wash all cookware and serving pieces that you haven't used recently.
- ◯ Label serving dishes with intended menu item.
- ◯ Tidy up living and dining rooms. Finish decorating.
- ◯ Thoroughly clean the bathroom guests will be using.
- ◯ Iron table linens and polish silver.
- ◯

Tuesday

- ◯ Move the turkey to the refrigerator to defrost.
- ◯ Place the turkey in the coldest area with a pan underneath to catch drips.
- ◯ Move frozen dishes to the refrigerator.
- ◯ Make cranberry sauce, breads, rolls, and pie crusts.
- ◯ Clean vegetables and refrigerate. Store in sealed plastic bag.
- ◯ Finalize your cooking schedule for Thursday.
- ◯ Shop for perishable groceries, fresh flowers, and remaining items.
- ◯ Do a spot cleaning of entertaining rooms.
- ◯ Make space for guest's coats and shoes.
- ◯

Wednesday

- ◯ Make your pies and other desserts.
- ◯ Make side dishes that will reheat well.
- ◯ Prep any vegetables, toppings, garnishes and stuffing ingredients.
- ◯ Set up the bar and chill the wine.
- ◯ Set the dining table. Arrange the chairs.
- ◯ Set out flowers, candles and other decorations.
- ◯

Notes

Kitchen checklist

Turkey Essentials

- ○ Roasting Pan
- ○ Roasting Rack
- ○ Carving Set
- ○ Carving Board
- ○ Cheesecloth
- ○ Brining Bags
- ○ Butcher's Twine
- ○
- ○ Oven Thermometer
- ○ Meat Thermometer
- ○ Bulb Baster
- ○ Flavor Injector
- ○ Turkey Lifters
- ○ Fine Mesh Strainer
- ○ Gravy Separator
- ○

Kitchen Tools

- ○ Saucepans
- ○ Wooden spoon
- ○ Slotted spoon
- ○ Flat Whisk
- ○ Paring knife
- ○ Vegetable Peeler
- ○ Tongs
- ○ Mandoline Slicer
- ○
- ○
- ○ Dry Measuring cups
- ○ Liquid Measuring cups
- ○ Grater
- ○ Colander
- ○ Potato masher
- ○ Food Processor
- ○ Blender
- ○ Stand Mixer
- ○ Hand Mixer
- ○

Bakeware

- ○ Pie Dishes
- ○ Casserole Dishes
- ○ Baking Sheets
- ○ Wire Cooling Racks
- ○ Mixing Bowls
- ○ Spatulas
- ○
- ○ Hand sifter
- ○ Rolling pin
- ○ Oven Mitts
- ○ Apron
- ○ Pie Server
- ○
- ○

Shopping List

- ○
- ○
- ○
- ○
- ○
- ○
- ○
- ○
- ○
- ○
- ○
- ○
- ○
- ○
- ○
- ○
- ○
- ○
- ○
- ○
- ○
- ○
- ○
- ○
- ○
- ○
- ○
- ○
- ○
- ○

Notes

Table & Bar *checklist*

Dinnerware
- ☐ Dinner Plates
- ☐ Bread Plates
- ☐ Salad/Dessert Plates
- ☐
- ☐ Bowls
- ☐ Cups and Saucers
- ☐ Chargers
- ☐

Drinkware
- ☐ Red Wine Glasses
- ☐ White Wine Glasses
- ☐ Wine Carafe
- ☐ Cork Screw
- ☐ Wine Stoppers
- ☐ Ice Bucket
- ☐ Water Glasses
- ☐ Highball Glasses
- ☐ Water Pitcher
- ☐ Bar Tool Set
- ☐ Coasters
- ☐

Flatware
- ☐ 5 piece Settings
- ☐ Serving Spoons
- ☐ Serving Forks
- ☐ Ladle
- ☐ Dessert Server
- ☐ Steak Knives
- ☐ Chef's Knife
- ☐ Bread Knife
- ☐ Cheese Knife
- ☐

Serving
- ☐ Turkey Platter
- ☐ Serving Bowls
- ☐ Serving Platters
- ☐ Salad Bowl
- ☐ Soup Tureen
- ☐ Serving Trays
- ☐ Condiment Dishes
- ☐
- ☐
- ☐ Trivets
- ☐ Butter Dish
- ☐ Gravy Boat
- ☐ Bread Basket
- ☐ Sugar & Creamer Set
- ☐ Salt & Pepper Shakers
- ☐ Cheese Board
- ☐
- ☐

Shopping List
- ☐
- ☐
- ☐
- ☐
- ☐
- ☐
- ☐
- ☐
- ☐
- ☐
- ☐
- ☐
- ☐
- ☐
- ☐
- ☐
- ☐
- ☐
- ☐
- ☐
- ☐
- ☐
- ☐
- ☐
- ☐
- ☐
- ☐
- ☐
- ☐
- ☐
- ☐
- ☐

Notes

October

Sunday	Monday	Tuesday	Wednesday	Thursday	Friday	Saturday

Notes

October

Sunday	Monday	Tuesday	Wednesday	Thursday	Friday	Saturday

Notes

October

Sunday	Monday	Tuesday	Wednesday	Thursday	Friday	Saturday

Notes

Notes

November

Sunday	Monday	Tuesday	Wednesday	Thursday	Friday	Saturday

Notes

November

Sunday	Monday	Tuesday	Wednesday	Thursday	Friday	Saturday

Notes

November

Sunday	Monday	Tuesday	Wednesday	Thursday	Friday	Saturday

Notes

Notes

Thanksgiving Week *planner*

Friday	Saturday	Sunday

Monday	Tuesday	Wednesday

Thursday	Notes	Give Thanks

Notes

Thanksgiving Week planner

Friday	Saturday	Sunday
Monday	Tuesday	Wednesday
Thursday	Notes	Give Thanks

Notes

Thanksgiving Week *planner*

Friday	Saturday	Sunday

Monday	Tuesday	Wednesday

Thursday	Notes	Give Thanks

Notes

Thanksgiving Week planner

Friday	Saturday	Sunday

Monday	Tuesday	Wednesday

Thursday	Notes	Give Thanks

Notes

Thanksgiving Week *planner*

Friday	Saturday	Sunday

Monday	Tuesday	Wednesday

Thursday	Notes	Give Thanks

Notes

Weekly agenda

Schedule

☐ Monday

☐ Tuesday

☐ Wednesday

☐ Thursday

☐ Friday

☐ Saturday

☐ Sunday

To-Do

Notes

Notes

Weekly agenda

Schedule

☐ Monday

☐ Tuesday

☐ Wednesday

☐ Thursday

☐ Friday

☐ Saturday

☐ Sunday

To-Do

Notes

Notes

Weekly agenda

Schedule

- [ ] Monday
- [ ] Tuesday
- [ ] Wednesday
- [ ] Thursday
- [ ] Friday
- [ ] Saturday
- [ ] Sunday

To-Do

Notes

Notes

Weekly agenda

Schedule

☐ Monday

☐ Tuesday

☐ Wednesday

☐ Thursday

☐ Friday

☐ Saturday

☐ Sunday

To-Do

Notes

Notes

Weekly agenda

Schedule

- Monday
- Tuesday
- Wednesday
- Thursday
- Friday
- Saturday
- Sunday

To-Do

Notes

Notes

Four Week checklist

Week 1	Week 2	Week 3

| Week 4 ||||
Sunday	Monday	Tuesday	Wednesday

| Thanksgiving Day |||
Morning	Midday	1 Hour Before Dinner

Notes

Four Week checklist

Week 1	Week 2	Week 3

Week 4

Sunday	Monday	Tuesday	Wednesday

Thanksgiving Day

Morning	Midday	1 Hour Before Dinner

Notes

Four Week checklist

Week 1	Week 2	Week 3

Week 4

Sunday	Monday	Tuesday	Wednesday

Thanksgiving Day

Morning	Midday	1 Hour Before Dinner

Notes

Four Week checklist

Week 1	Week 2	Week 3

Week 4

Sunday	Monday	Tuesday	Wednesday

Thanksgiving Day

Morning	Midday	1 Hour Before Dinner

Notes

Four Week *checklist*

Week 1	Week 2	Week 3

Week 4

Sunday	Monday	Tuesday	Wednesday

Thanksgiving Day

Morning	Midday	1 Hour Before Dinner

Notes

Cleaning checklist

Kitchen

- ○ Wipe down lights fixtures and fans.
- ○ Wipe down the cabinets.
- ○ Clean out refrigerator and freezer.
- ○ Clean microwave, stove, and oven.
- ○ Clear and clean counters.
- ○ Wipe down appliances.
- ○ Clean and organize pantry.
- ○ Sweep and mop the floor.

Dining Room

- ○ Wipe off marks on doors and walls.
- ○ Clean light fixtures and fans.
- ○ Wipe down mirrors and glass.
- ○ Dust furniture and decor.
- ○ Wipe down and polish table.
- ○ Wipe down chairs.
- ○ Wipe down baseboards.
- ○ Vacuum and/or mop the floor.

Living/Family Rooms

- ○ Wipe off marks on doors and walls.
- ○ Clean light fixtures and fans.
- ○ Wipe down mirrors and glass.
- ○ Dust furniture and decor.
- ○ Wipe down electronics.
- ○ Wipe down baseboards.
- ○ Vacuum and/or mop the floor.

Guest Room

- ○ Change and wash linens.
- ○ Dust furniture and decor.
- ○ Wipe down mirrors and glass.
- ○ Vacuum and mop the floor.
- ○ Add a special touch to welcome guests.

Entry/Front Porch

- ○ Clear any cobwebs and leaves.
- ○ Wipe down the doorframe.
- ○ Clean light fixtures and glass.
- ○ Shake door mat.
- ○ Hang a seasonal wreath on the front door.

Bathrooms

- ○ Wash shower curtains and rugs.
- ○ Scrub shower, sink, and toilet.
- ○ Wipe down mirrors and glass.
- ○ Wipe down counters.
- ○ Put out fresh towels and candles.
- ○ Stock with extra soap and toilet paper.
- ○ Sweep and mop floor.

Shopping list

Decorations

Table Linens & Accessories

Kitchen Items

Table & Bar Items

Non-Perishables

Household & Paper Goods

Notes

Shopping list

Decorations

Table Linens & Accessories

Kitchen Items

Table & Bar Items

None-Perishables

Household & Paper Goods

Notes

Shopping list

Decorations

Table Linens & Accessories

Kitchen Items

Table & Bar Items

None-Perishables

Household & Paper Goods

Notes

Grocery list

Notes

Grocery list

Notes

Grocery list

Notes

Grocery list

Notes

Grocery list

Notes

Budget tracker

Item	Budgeted	Actual	Difference

Budget tracker

Item	Budgeted	Actual	Difference

Budget tracker

Item	Budgeted	Actual	Difference

Budget tracker

Item	Budgeted	Actual	Difference

Budget tracker

Item	Budgeted	Actual	Difference

Notes

Cooking plan

Main Course:

Appetizers & Sides

Desserts:

Drinks:

Ingredients List:

Cooking plan

Main Course:

Appetizers & Sides

Desserts:

Drinks:

Ingredients List:

Cooking plan

Main Course:

Appetizers & Sides:

Desserts:

Drinks:

Ingredients List:

Cooking plan

Main Course:

Appetizers & Sides

Desserts:

Drinks:

Ingredients List:

Cooking plan

Main Course:

Appetizers & Sides

Desserts:

Drinks:

Ingredients List:

Notes

Menu planner

MENU

Appetizers

Main Course

Side Dishes

Casseroles

Drinks

Desserts

Shopping list

Notes

Menu planner

MENU

Appetizers

Main Course

Side Dishes

Casseroles

Drinks

Desserts

Shopping list

Notes

Menu planner

MENU

Appetizers

Main Course

Side Dishes

Casseroles

Drinks

Desserts

Shopping list

Notes

Menu planner

MENU

Appetizers

Main Course

Side Dishes

Casseroles

Drinks

Desserts

Shopping list

Notes

Menu planner

MENU

Appetizers

Main Course

Side Dishes

Casseroles

Drinks

Desserts

Shopping List

Notes

Master Ingredient list

Master Ingredient list

Master Ingredient list

Master Ingredient list

Master Ingredient list

Thanksgiving Day Cooking *schedule*

Thanksgiving meal served at:

Time	What Needs To Be Done?
7:00 a.m.	
8:00 a.m.	
9:00 a.m.	
10:00 a.m.	
11:00 a.m.	
12:00 p.m.	
1:00 p.m.	
2:00 p.m.	
3:00 p.m.	
4:00 p.m.	
5:00 p.m.	
6:00 p.m.	
7:00 p.m.	
8:00 p.m.	
9:00 p.m.	

Thanksgiving Day Cooking
schedule

Thanksgiving meal served at:

Time	What Needs To Be Done?
7:00 a.m.	
8:00 a.m.	
9:00 a.m.	
10:00 a.m.	
11:00 a.m.	
12:00 p.m.	
1:00 p.m.	
2:00 p.m.	
3:00 p.m.	
4:00 p.m.	
5:00 p.m.	
6:00 p.m.	
7:00 p.m.	
8:00 p.m.	
9:00 p.m.	

Thanksgiving Day Cooking
schedule

Thanksgiving meal served at:

Time	What Needs To Be Done?
7:00 a.m.	
8:00 a.m.	
9:00 a.m.	
10:00 a.m.	
11:00 a.m.	
12:00 p.m.	
1:00 p.m.	
2:00 p.m.	
3:00 p.m.	
4:00 p.m.	
5:00 p.m.	
6:00 p.m.	
7:00 p.m.	
8:00 p.m.	
9:00 p.m.	

Notes

Cooking Time *table*

Dinner Time: Guests: Turkey LBS: Cook Time:

Menu Item	Cook Method	Ready Time	Cook Time	Begin Cook	Prep Time	Begin Prep

Cooking Time *table*

| Dinner Time: | Guests: | Turkey LBS: | Cook Time: |

Menu Item	Cook Method	Ready Time	Cook Time	Begin Cook	Prep Time	Begin Prep

Cooking Time *table*

Dinner Time: Guests: Turkey LBS: Cook Time:

Menu Item	Cook Method	Ready Time	Cook Time	Begin Cook	Prep Time	Begin Prep

Notes

Table, Décor & seating

The Dining Table

| Tables: # | Chairs: # | ○ Formal ○ Informal |

Linens & Accessories

- ○ Table cloth
- ○ Table runner
- ○ Napkins
- ○ Napkin Rings
- ○ Vases
- ○ Place Cards
- ○ Candlesticks
- ○ Candles

Centerpiece

Other Table Décor

Informal

Utensils are placed one inch from the edge of the table

Formal

Cup and saucer generally aren't placed on the table until the dessert course

Seating Arrangement

Notes

Guest list

RSVP	Guest	Bringing	Requests	Adults	Children
☐					
☐					
☐					
☐					
☐					
☐					
☐					
☐					
☐					
☐					
☐					
☐					
☐					
☐					
☐					
☐					
☐					
☐					
☐					
☐					
☐					
☐					
☐					
☐					
☐					

Guest list

RSVP	Guest	Bringing	Requests	Adults	Children
☐					
☐					
☐					
☐					
☐					
☐					
☐					
☐					
☐					
☐					
☐					
☐					
☐					
☐					
☐					
☐					
☐					
☐					
☐					
☐					
☐					
☐					
☐					
☐					
☐					
☐					
☐					
☐					

Guest list

RSVP	Guest	Bringing	Requests	Adults	Children
☐					
☐					
☐					
☐					
☐					
☐					
☐					
☐					
☐					
☐					
☐					
☐					
☐					
☐					
☐					
☐					
☐					
☐					
☐					
☐					
☐					
☐					
☐					
☐					
☐					
☐					
☐					

Notes

Notes

Notes

Notes

Notes

Notes

Notes

Memories

Memories

Memories

Memories

Memories

Memories

www.ingramcontent.com/pod-product-compliance
Lightning Source LLC
Chambersburg PA
CBHW081154070526
44583CB00021B/2833